Identity Unveiled

IDENTITY UNVEILED

DAUGHTER
OF THE
KING OF KINGS

Reflections on God's Grace

Shirene H. Gentry

library partners press
a digital publishing imprint

Winston-Salem | North Carolina | Beaufort

ISBN 978-1-61846-082-0 (paperback)

http://hopeunveiled.com

Original photos used with permission

TEXT Forum
DISPLAY Papyrus

Produced and Distributed By:
    Library Partners Press
    ZSR Library
    Wake Forest University
    1834 Wake Forest Road
    Winston-Salem, North Carolina 27106

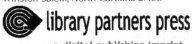

a digital publishing imprint
www.librarypartnerspress.org
Winston-Salem | North Carolina | Beaufort

Manufactured in the United States of America

CONTENTS

MY JOURNEY OF DISCOVERY

All of my family of origin passed away by 2001, but in 2017, I looked at the massive paper trail left by my grandmother, mother, and father. For the first time, I discovered that the story of my adoption did not match the mountain of evidence set before me. I believe that the circumstantial evidence points to one conclusion: that I am an illegitimate daughter of the deposed *shahanshah* ("king of kings") of Iran, Mohammad Reza Pahlavi. This startling discovery caused me to ask myself this question: ***What would I think of myself if I really were the daughter of Mohammad Reza Pahlavi?***

- *Would I look at myself differently?*
- *Would others treat me differently?*
- *Would I walk a little more confidently?*
- *Would I consider myself a person of worth and value?*

Furthermore, I began to think of this concept within a spiritual context. If you and I are daughters of THE King of Kings, what is our identity? What destroys it? How can it be reclaimed? How can we walk through life with value and worth no matter what this imperfect world may unexpectedly give us?

This book is designed to answer these questions while celebrating the totality of who you and I are in relation to our Creator.

ACKNOWLEDGMENTS

To Jimmy Tomlin and Bob Buckley, I thank you for sharing my story through your respective journalistic mediums.

To Susan Bradley, editor extraordinaire, I thank you for your professional coaching and editing.

To Suzanne Mikkelson, I thank you for reading this manuscript and offering spiritual insights.

To Bill Kane at my alma mater, Wake Forest University, I thank you for formatting and publishing this work.

To the men in my life—my husband and sons—you are my princes.

Lastly, to my King of Kings, I will live the remainder of my life in complete gratitude for what you have done and continue to do in my life. Your eye saw even me, unborn and unplanned, as your love reached down to orchestrate every detail of my life— the people, the timing, and the actions. I am in awe!

And yet, the God of heaven and earth looked down upon a little girl lost in a Persian kingdom. The worst trauma that could possibly happen to a child and said, 'I choose you. I choose you. Not just in spite of what you've been through, but strangely, oddly, also in the providence and sovereignty of God because of it.'

Beth Moore, *Esther*

DEDICATION

This book is dedicated to the memory of my mother and any woman who questions her worth, value, and purpose. May the truths set forth in this book clarify, once and for all, that your identity is not based on performance, a negative life event, "likes," impression management, or comparison. Nor is it based on the faulty voices of others or critical words you tell yourself.

My prayer is that my family story will encourage you in your life journey. May the chapters that you rewrite of your life story bring God glory.

To my dear mom, I miss you more now than ever before. If only I had known. One day we will walk the streets of gold together. Until then, may God use our stories to demonstrate how he pursued us relentlessly, regardless of how our paths took us to the foot of the cross.

Amen.

THREE FATHERS

A long time ago, in a land far away,
The shahanshah *(king of kings) reigned.*
This is the story of three fathers . . .

one couldn't say "no"
one decided to say "yes"
One was author of all.

one was dejected at my birth
one was delighted at my birth
One had always planned my birth.

one acted cowardly
one acted courageously
One orchestrated confidently.

one declared me illegitimate
one decided me legitimate
One divinely calls me His.

one lived in secrecy
one labored selflessly
One reigns supremely.

one fled in exile
one fought extravagantly
One fights for me.

one called me nameless
one gave me his name
One calls me by name!

days ordained for me
were written in your book
before one of them
be.

INTRODUCTION

For most of my life, I believed one story about my early life that shaped how I viewed myself. Now, having learned that story was very likely untrue, I have had to reconsider who I am in the light of this new knowledge. You, too, may be living with a mistaken identity that was never meant to be yours. Do not be one day late in taking hold of your true identity and walking in the truth of who God says you really are—a daughter of the King of Kings!

Mistaken Identity.

She made a sw[eet?]
[p]icture as she st[ood]
[i]n the doorway o[f]
[l]ittle mountain
[h]ouse.

Oh yes you ha[ve]
[pa]ssed already [the?]
[lik]e the little s[?]
[he]r eyes were
[sh]aded violet
[?]d t[?]

Jelia Staton.
English grade till
"Miss J. class 2.15.
one day late.

Part 1

WHO AM I?

Chapter One

MASTERPIECE

For you created my inmost being; you knit me together in my mother's womb. I praise you because I am fearfully and wonderfully made; your works are wonderful, I know that full well. My frame was not hidden from you when I was made in the secret place. When I was woven together in the depths of the earth, your eyes saw my unformed body. All the days ordained for me were written in your book before one of them came to be.

Psalm 139:13–16

Hardwired in our DNA is the desire to know who we are and where we came from. The recent spike in genetic testing confirms this. Have you ever asked yourself, "Who am I?" I never did for many years. Then the results of my DNA tests refuted the facts my adoptive parents had told me my entire life about my parentage. Instead of being the offspring of an Iranian father and a European or American mother, I found out that I was 99.3% Persian. The story I had long believed was now refuted.

What Identifies You: Your Thumbprint
Take a look at your thumbprint. Did you know that throughout history, you have been the only person to bear this unique configuration of loops, whorls, and arches? This pattern was developed three months before you were born. Identical twins do not even share the same thumbprint. The three layers of skin—epidermis, dermis, and hypodermis—buckle because the basal layer grows faster than the

others, thus causing your one-of-a-kind print. There has never been nor ever will be another you.

SNPs

I was fascinated when my DNA testing company sent the raw data describing my genetic configurations. Single Nucleotide Polymorphisms (SNPs) are the variations in the DNA code that make each of us unique. Normally, in cell division, the DNA of one cell is exactly replicated in the new cell. Sometimes, however, the copying process is not exact, resulting in unique variations—SNPs—that are passed along to descendants and serve as strong indicators of familial connections. Viewing the raw data and the complexity such findings represent is nothing short of awe-inspiring.

Because I am adopted and the identity of my birth parents has never been disclosed, I have never been able to look at another individual and see my image reflected in him or her as an indicator of our shared DNA. Many times, I have looked at my grown sons to see how we share physical characteristics—a fascination of mine as their biological mother with whom they share DNA.

The truth is that none of us has control over what makes up our physical being. The unique components that define who we are result from God working through nature's handiwork. In a biological sense, and in every other sense as well, God knows who my birth parents are. The evidence put forth in this book is all circumstantial, but it adds up to make a strong case as to my physical origin and paternal lineage. To date, I still have no indication as to the identity of my birth mother. As the above-referenced verses indicate, God knows her even if I never will. He knows her name, her story, her backstory, and her choices, including her choice (or not) to be with the king. Perhaps she had no say in the matter. Perhaps she did. Regardless, I was woven together in the secret place with my Creator knowing every detail and knowing me before I was formed. Isn't this thought gloriously incomprehensible?

I entered this world with what sociologists call "ascribed" labels—the labels that a person has no control over. My labels were "unplanned," "unwanted," and "illegitimate." Although these were fitting labels for an illegitimate infant, God had already given me the best label: daughter of the King. I know this statement to be true:

What man calls a mistake, God calls a masterpiece.

Sister and daughter of the King of Kings, remember that you are a masterpiece, fearfully and wonderfully made. There is nothing about how you were conceived or any detail about your life that is unseen by the One who created you.

God's Timing Unveiled: The Story Unravels

When it came to the story of my early life, why would I ever have questioned my adoptive mother? I never had a reason to doubt that what she told me was true. I'm thankful that I always knew I was born in Tehran and that I was adopted. Any information tendered was always from my mother, never my father. The story she gave me was vague: my birth mother may have been French and my father was Iranian. She also said I was a twin and that my birth mother and twin died during childbirth. I was told my biological father died in an earthquake one month prior to my birth. Indeed, there was an earthquake in Tehran in September 1962, the month before I was born. This is the story I believed for the first thirty-eight years of my life. The first red flag came, ironically, on my birthday in 2000. But I was in the throes of caregiving for my aging parents while my husband and I were busy raising two small children. It was not the time to focus on me.

Now that I look back on my father's lack of disclosure, I am convinced that my mother made an impulsive decision to adopt me while she was on a trip to Tehran. This was before she and Dad went together, as his military departure documents indicate.

What evidence points to my conclusion? First, I have evidence that she attended a Gulf District Wives Club fashion show on February 24, 1962.

I have reason to believe that she made this trip without my father, because his military documentation indicates that he (and Mom) were to leave for his Tehran assignment on December 12, 1962. Dad was a lieutenant colonel in the United States Army, and the unofficial order from the Pentagon that precipitated his assignment in Iran was dated October 10, 1962, one day before my birth.

It was during my mother's solo trip in February 1962 that she became acquainted with other military wives in the Gulf District Wives Club. Those women would have helped her acclimate to what would be her new environment, even before my parents' official arrival. I speculate she learned of a single, pregnant woman who was looking to give up an unwanted baby. At that time, Iran did not honor international adoption, so the details and the people involved would have been veiled in secrecy.

My father was assigned as the commanding officer of the 64th Engineering Battalion. Accordingly, his circle of influence and acquaintance would have included others of high rank and position in both the Iranian and American societal circles.

Why do I believe my adoption was prearranged before my birth? It is because of handwritten information on the backs of photographs left in my parents' paper trail. The comments on the back of these photos were written by my mother.

Since I was not born until October 11, my mother's notation about September in the following photo indicates that the details of my adoption were being negotiated before my birth.

"Clipper Party"

C.O. of 64th Engineer
Lt. Col. Daniel Hutzko
Sept. 1962

Month he became a
Dad in Persia!

Additional hints are disclosed on the back of this photograph of my mother (at right) and Charlotte Peters, a TV personality at the St. Louis station where Mom worked:

This evidence from three weeks after my birth indicates that Mom had already named me! As I will share later, I have no birth certificate, and the only paper that discloses any information about me (a certificate of identity) was not even produced until seven months after my birth. That certificate is written in Farsi.

Although my adoption was prearranged, it is unclear as to why there was a seven-month gap between my birth (October 11, 1962) and the time I went home to live with my adoptive parents. This lag is evidenced by a handwritten letter from my mother to my grandmother on May 10, 1963. The letter describes how Mom was busy buying baby items in expectation of bringing me home on Mother's Day weekend.

I speculate that during the seven months between my birth and my adoption, I was being cared for in the shah's palace. Author Fereydoun Hoveyda writes the following in his book, *The Fall of the Shah*:

> *Despite an outward display of unity there was no love lost between the members of this royal family, who were not all children of the same mother. Inside the court circles they sniped at each other more or less openly, and I often observed backbiting at parties, with amusement to begin with, but later with dismay at the thought of the way their rivalries affected the affairs of the country. Every prince and princess kept a small court and a larger entourage, and ill-feeling proliferated among their courtiers like the ripples from a thrown pebble* (p. 136).

This excerpt substantiates that children of the shah's various liaisons were being raised together in the palace. I wonder if an invitation and photographs my mother had saved also corroborate the above-referenced paragraph. The invitation was for a second birthday party for Princess Alavi at a home in Tehran. At the time my mother and I attended this party, I was fifteen months old and had been living with Mom and Dad for eight months. (Mom and I are seated at left on the sofa.)

The strongest evidence supporting my connection to the royal family is a letter sent by Major General Eugene Salet, United States Ground Forces Commander, to my mother on April 29, 1964. (See letter on page 22. General Salet is pictured at left in the accompanying photograph; the shah is at right.)

Note the last paragraph of General Salet's letter in which he indicates that showing me the enclosed photograph would "create a trauma." I infer that he is referencing the emotional attachment that results between an infant and a parent. If I had never been in the shah's presence, then I would have no reaction—positive or negative—to viewing a photograph of him. Another piece of evidence supporting my belief that Mom impulsively decided on her own to adopt me is that this letter is addressed only to her and not to both of my parents.

29 April 1964

Dear Diane:

Thank you so much for the tape and for your note.
I hope that the taped interview proved interesting
"For the Girls". I, too, enjoyed doing this bit and I
felt that it turned out very well.

Please tell everyone on the staff that it was nice
to meet them and that I do hope to see them again. Rest
assured that my memories of Teheran are truly good ones;
particularly when one is exposed to people such as you,
Dan, and others of like caliber.

My trip home was indeed most pleasant. I stopped
in Paris for three days and ate my way through several
restaurants. The first day was devoted to recouping lost
strength and the remainder of my stay was, as I said, devoted to hunting up fine cuisine. Paris is indeed beautiful at this time of the year. I am always thrilled to
see the city, particularly during the Springtime.

I am inclosing copies of the pictures taken with
the Shah. I suggest you do not show them to your beautiful little girl since they might create a trauma.

Please pass my warm regards to Dan and warm
personal regards to you.

Sincerely,

EUGENE A. SALET
Major General, USA

Really only one
picture - not plural.
Let me know how
things are going
re: Athenian
Custody of etc.

Mrs. Diane Hritzko
U. S. Military Assistance Advisory Group to Iran
APO 205
New York, New York

As I mentioned, a certificate documenting my birth was issued when I was seven months old. I believe this paperwork was fabricated in an attempt to cover up my true identity and protect the people involved.

The following document, signed by Farman Farmaian, is not corroborated by the photographs, letters, and handwritten information I have included here.

آموزشگاه خدمات اجتماعی

Oct. 27, 1964

TEHERAN SCHOOL OF SOCIAL WORK

October 27, 1964

TO WHOM IT MAY CONCERN:

This is to certify that the case of Firoozeh Kavian Monfared was brought to the attention of the Family Aid Society of the Teheran School of Social Work as an abandoned child. The child had been deposited at the Women's Hospital since birth. She had been there six months and no one had claimed her. The Teheran School of Social Work assigned a social worker to investigate the case and after exhaustive search no trace of parents could be found. The child was therefore declared an orphan and in May 1963 was given to Colonel and Mrs. Daniel Hritzko for care and proper upbringing and possible adoption.

(Miss) Sattareh Farman-Farmaian,
Director,
Teheran School of Social Work
Post Office Box 2851
Teheran, Iran.

Another small sheet of paper found in my grandmother's possessions shows the information she scribbled about what the prepared story was going to be about the details of my birth and adoption. No doubt her notes were written during a long-distance telephone call from my mother in Tehran to her home in Lynchburg, Virginia. The notes say that my birth mother was French and my father was Iranian. At the bottom of the page, Grandma wrote a name that I believe is the first name of an Iranian national whom I met five years ago in the United Kingdom. He disclosed that my father was a "high-ranking Iranian" and my mother was American. My recent DNA tests place the likelihood of having an American mother in doubt, however. As previously indicated, my genetic reports indicate that I am 99.3% Persian. Unless such an American had only Persian heritage herself, it seems impossible that my genetic makeup could be as it is. This man, who was clearly trying to keep me from the truth about my birth parents, insisted repeatedly that "it doesn't matter the life you've had and what's in the past. All that matters is your life now."

He knows the whole story, and with a shred of truth, he disclosed an untruth to sidetrack the whole truth. Why? I believe it is an attempt to cover for my Iranian birth mother, who may still be alive. Or perhaps it is to protect the royal family. Why he was instrumental in my adoption process is still unclear. My mother made his acquaintance during her solo trip before she and Dad arrived in Iran in December 1962.

A postscript at the top of a June 1964 letter typed by my father to Mom while he was working in Libya indicated Mom had been in meetings in Tehran with Ms. Farmaian and Dr. Mahmoud Espandiary. The former was the director of the Tehran School of Social Work, founded in 1958 and partly funded by the shah. She herself was a princess, and she and the shah were well acquainted.

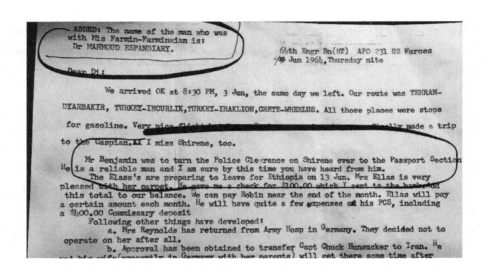

ADDED: The name of the man who was with Mis Farmin-Farmineian is: Dr MAHMOUD ESPANDIARY.

6bth Engr Bn(HT) APO 231 US Forces
/# Jun 1964,Thursday nite

Dear Di:

We arrived OK at 8:30 PM, 3 Jun, the same day we left. Our route was TEHRAN-DYARBAKIR, TURKEY-INCURLIK,TURKEY-IRAKLION,CRETE-WHEELUS. All those places were stops for gasoline. Very nice flight _____ finally made a trip to the Caspian. IX I miss Shirene, too.

Mr Benjamin was to turn the Police Clearance on Shirene over to the Passport Section He is a reliable man and I am sure by this time you have heard from him.
The Elass's are preparing to leave for Ethiopia on 13 Jun. Mrs Ellas is very pleased with her carpet. He gave me a check for $100.00 which I sent to the bank. Add this total to our balance. We can pay Robin near the end of the month. Ellas will pay a certain amount each month. He will have quite a few expenses on his PCS, including a $400.00 Commissary deposit.
Following other things have developed:
a. Mrs Reynolds has returned from Army Hosp in Germany. They decided not to operate on her after all.
b. Approval has been obtained to transfer Capt Chuck Hunsucker to Iran. He and his wife(presently in Germany with her parents) will get there some time after

Another interesting component can be found in Google content that enables me to compare my photograph with one of the royal family.

At left below is the shah's twin sister, Princess Ashraf Pahlavi. I am pictured at right at a comparable age.

As I was completing this book, I unearthed another piece of evidence as to my possible heritage, which came in the form of a gold ring that the Iranian national gave my mother in the 1960s when we lived in Germany. In the years since I have possessed the ring, I had never noticed that the image of a crown was stamped on the inside. I showed a photo of the ring to two Iranian friends who had lived in Iran during the reign of the shah, and they confirmed without a doubt that it was the insignia of the shah and the Pahlavi family. I can't think of a reason my mother would have been given the ring except for a significant connection to the royal family. The outside of the ring is pictured below.

Learning that the facts of my early life differ from what I had always been told came as a shock to me. Gaining this knowledge has caused me to think about who I am in relation to my heavenly Father—the one whose parentage is never in question and who will never abandon or forsake me. Each of us can benefit by reflecting on who we are in God's sight—chosen and dearly loved!

Unveiling a Spiritual Takeaway

Let the verses in Psalm 139 penetrate your heart and mind. Here are the implications of this Scripture within **your** personal backstory:

- God knew you before you were born.
- God knew the exact day you would be conceived, which marked your entrance into humanity.
- Your life has a personal backstory with people and places that are uniquely yours.
- God orchestrated the events in your family of origin so that the timing of your birth coincided with their choices, whether they acknowledged Him or not.
- Because of your unique thumbprint and genetic combination, there will never be another you.
- The beginning—YOUR beginning—is not the ending!

Chapter Two

GOD-IMAGE: YOUR SPIRITUAL DNA

So God created man in his own image, in the image of God he created him; male and female he created them.
Genesis 1:27

For he chose us in him before the creation of the world to be holy and blameless in his sight. In love he predestined us to be adopted as his sons through Jesus Christ, in accordance with his pleasure and will—to the praise of his glorious grace, which he has freely given us in the One he loves. . . . In him we were also chosen, having been predestined according to the plan of him who works out everything in conformity with the purpose of his will, in order that we, who were the first to hope in Christ, might be for the praise of his glory.
Ephesians 1:4–6, 11–12

There are no gradations of the image of God.
Martin Luther King Jr.

Woven deep into your being is the image of God. This immensely dense truth is pregnant with implications that give you worth. The Greek translation for "worth" is *axios,* which means "of weight and worth." In biblical times, gold and other precious metals were placed on a balancing scale where their worth was determined by their weight, leading to the expression "worth their weight in gold" (Lamentations 4:20).

Bearing the image of God distinguishes us humans from the rest of creation. Specifically, it is reasoning, intellect, dominion, creativity, and will that make us the pinnacle of His creation. Although this image has been damaged by original sin, it is not destroyed.

Ideally, we operate from the understanding that we have been created in God's image. In addition, each of us is affected by our self-image—the perception or mental picture that we have of our appearance, abilities, and personal worth. This includes, but is not limited to, a journey of self-discovery as to personal strengths and passions. We reflect God's image best when we are aware of our individual giftings, when the places of disappointment in our hearts have been healed, and when we recognize what he has redeemed in our lives.

Perhaps your self-image has been warped by criticism, disapproval, or pain. This, in turn, affects your ability to see yourself clearly. Your worth, value, and purpose have become damaged, and this is not God's intent for your life.

As a young child, I recall my parents telling me I was pretty. When the unsettling teen years arrived, however, I was living with my grandmother, who was doing everything she could to have a second chance at parenthood. More important daily priorities trumped the daily affirmations I needed to promote self-acceptance.

As a teenager in the 1970s, my self-image was anything but healthy. I could not accept the notion that I was formed in God's image, because I could not get beyond the reflection in the mirror. There wasn't one physical or personality trait I liked. Not one. I was too tall, my hair was too bushy, my nose was too big, my personality was too introverted, and my athletic abilities were nonexistent. Somehow, the "fearfully and wonderfully made" statement in Psalm 139 did not resonate in the depths of my soul.

As I will share later, by the time I reached the teenage years, my parents' marital, financial, and relational challenges did not leave room for a teenage girl to hear the much-needed affirmation that only parents can give. My mother tried to calm my teenage self-loathing by reassuring me that plastic surgery was always an option when I became old enough.

My lack of involvement in school activities meant that I was slow to discover my strengths and abilities. This, in turn, caused me to flounder in self-discovery, resulting in my perception that I wasn't of much value or worth. My only involvement in extracurricular activities came in the form of piano and dance. Although both are intrinsically worthwhile and I am thankful for what they taught me, the motives for taking lessons were not my own. My grandmother always wanted my mother to take piano lessons, so raising me gave her a second chance to live out this wish. Similarly, I took dance lessons because my mother had always wanted them for herself.

Whether it was physical looks or personality traits and abilities, my self-image was warped. I longed to be someone I wasn't. It did not help that the popular girls in high school appeared to be the antithesis of who I was: short, blonde, and extroverted. I always felt like I was on the outskirts of the popular crowd.

I learned quickly that my worth came from doing well in school. This pattern continued through college. My grandmother framed every dean's list certificate I earned during my undergraduate studies. Although I could have chosen a harder area of study, I still relied on performance to be the barometer of my worth and value. The positive flip side was that my family allowed me to study what truly interested me.

When your self-image is damaged, you cannot accurately view yourself as God sees you. If you go through life being weighed down by a flawed self-image, your ability to accurately reflect God's image in your life is thwarted.

A positive correlation exists between your self-image and the image of God that you portray to the world. As your self-perception becomes restored and renewed, so does the image of God that is reflected in your life.

As I reflect on my personal journey of self-worth, confidence, and value, it all began with the healing touch of God's hand on the deepest parts of my hurting heart. When His Spirit spoke truth into the recesses of my mind, confidence and value seemed to permeate my entire being. I began to accept my physical traits. My clothes and jewelry became more bold. I was transformed from the inside out and from the outside in! I've learned to focus on the physical traits I like, accept the ones I cannot or choose not to change, and accept that I am a work in progress for those aspects of my personality that evolve one degree at a time with the Holy Spirit's prompting (2 Corinthians 3:18).

When we draw closer to God, the Holy Spirit does an amazing work in our hearts and minds. Our view of others, our view of ourselves, and our view of God take dramatic shifts. In turn, we are able to connect with others on a deeper emotional level. Thus, our ability to reflect God's image in our lives sparks a greater spiritual understanding and connects us to others like never before.

The following chapters will address the cumulative effect of how a woman's self-image is damaged, how that affects her view of God, and how she is able to move forward into her God-ordained future!

Unveiling a Spiritual Takeaway

If the image of God in you has been damaged, take heart that it can be restored (2 Corinthians 3:18).

Chapter Three

BACKSTORY

A King and a Woman

Mohammad Reza Pahlavi, *shahanshah* ("king of kings"), became the ruler of the Persian Peacock Dynasty in 1941 after his father abdicated the throne. The younger Pahlavi was just shy of his twenty-second birthday.

At the time of my birth in October 1962, the king was married to his third wife, Empress Farah, with whom he had four children. She is still alive at the time of this writing. Two of their children are still living. His first marriage to an Egyptian princess, with whom he had a daughter, was relatively short-lived (nine years). His second marriage to Soraya Esfandiary-Bakhtiari was terminated after a few years, as she could not bear any children, thus producing no heirs to the throne. According to Persian and American friends living in Tehran during the 1960s, the shah had an inclination toward luxury cars and beautiful women.

An Iranian national, an individual who knows the whole story about my adoption, told me that my birth mother was "in her early twenties" at the time of my birth. She had become pregnant by a married man, a "high-ranking Iranian official." On the same day the Rev. Dr. Martin Luther King Jr. was delivering a speech to 2,200 students at Wait Chapel on the campus of Wake Forest University (my future alma mater), a young woman on the other side of the world entered a hospital and gave birth to a blue-eyed daughter. Dr. King's speech focused on the horrors of segregation and the potential for racial healing through integration. Meanwhile, God was integrating the lives of five people to make His plan come to fruition. I would later be identified on a certificate of identity as "Firoozeh," meaning *blue* or *turquoise* in Farsi. Sources have informed me that the shah held a love interest in a woman much younger than he around the time of my birth. Apparently, most people living in Tehran knew of this relationship even though it was supposed to remain a secret. I wonder if these two independent sources are referring to the same woman and, if so, could she be my birth mother?

A Socialite and a Soldier

On Thursday, December 1, 1960, a striking socialite met a dashing and decorated soldier at a bar in the Fort Myer Officers Club in Arlington, Virginia. He would recall many years later that he met his "blonde bombshell" that evening.

Daniel, the officer, was a lieutenant colonel in the U.S. Army. He was based in St. Louis as the army's liaison with the Aeronautical Chart and Information Center. He had already earned a Silver Star at the close of World War II while crossing the Rhine River under heavy combat fire, as well as other awards during his tours in Canada, Japan, and Korea. He had been previously married to a French woman at the close of World War II and had fathered a daughter who was named after his deceased mother (Karen Anna).

Dana, the socialite—preferring her pen name of Diane—had landed a job as the assistant editor for *American Youth* magazine, based in Arlington. She worked under the identity of Diane Byers, using her first husband's surname. She had married him near the end of World War II (July 1945) and had "abandoned" him in 1957, per their divorce decree.

Dan and Diane's whirlwind romance was spontaneous and impulsive. They were married by a justice of the peace in St. Louis, just seven weeks after they had met. Following their marriage, they lived in St. Louis until their military assignment in Tehran. Dan continued in his military capacity as the army liaison with the Aeronautical and Space program, while Diane worked for (then) KSD television as a producer and director. They had no biological children together, and I became their only adopted child.

Backward Glances

Zelia William Staton. My maternal grandmother was born in Amherst County, Virginia (then known as Sandidges), on April 1, 1904. Her parents were Pitt W. Staton and Eliza Campbell Staton. Zelia was the youngest of four daughters, having been preceded by Cora, Beulah, and Eva. The sons born to the marriage did not survive. Pitt and Eliza built a home on the acreage they owned. They raised their daughters there and became a respected family in the community. They were charter members of Emmanuel Baptist Church, founded on July 4, 1907, not far from the Staton residence. Below is a photograph of Zelia as a teenager.

A small schoolhouse built across the street from the church was where Zelia's older sisters went on to teach young students. Deciding to go a different career path than her sisters, Zelia completed her nursing training by age 18 and became employed by Lynchburg Hospital.

CITY OF LYNCHBURG

OFFICE OF

SUPERINTENDENT OF LYNCHBURG HOSPITAL

MISS M. F. COWLING
SUPERINTENDENT

Lynchburg, Va., June 14, 1922.

Miss Zelia W. Staton,
R. F. D.,
Sandidges, Va.

Dear Miss Staton:-

I have your letter of the 6th inst., and will expect you on September 1st.

I am enclosing you sample of goods for dresses, and kerchief and bib patterns.

Relative to bobbed hair, if your hair is already bobbed, it will be alright, but if not, I would not advise you to bob it, as it will be more trouble to wear a cap with bobbed hair.

Yours very truly,

MFC-H.
Encl.

Superintendent.

Five months after Zelia's nursing career began, her father died unexpectedly on November 3, 1922. It is thought that his death at the age of 50 was due to an unusual combination of pneumonia and gangrene.

Although he was well respected at the time of his passing, he could never escape a label that had been ascribed to him throughout his life and even after it: illegitimate. Family speculations abound as to the identity of his biological father.

Pursuant to this generation's mindset of dealing with secrets and labels, my grandmother never mentioned her father to me. Not his name, not his beginning, not his backstory, not his death, not her love for him. Nothing.

Did Zelia let her father's negative ascribed label shape her own identity? I suspect she did. Otherwise, she would have been able to discuss it freely. The same reality held true back then as it does now:

If you do not frame your identity to coincide with how God sees you, shame can cover a family for generations.

Either before Zelia's father died or sometime the same year, her path crossed with that of a traveling salesman named Sherman Edward McClellan. He was from Huntington, West Virginia, and unbeknownst to her, he had been married twice. His smooth-talking skills were used not only on his customers, but also on the women he courted.

The photo following shows Zelia's mother, Eliza (known as "Big Mama"), chaperoning a date with Sherman.

Being Chaperoned

My grandmother married Sherman McClellan on July 5, 1924, in Ironton, Ohio, perhaps while he was traveling as a clothes salesman spanning territory in West Virginia, Ohio, Kentucky, Virginia, Tennessee, and North Carolina. He earned $50 to $60 a week. He was also a professional poker player whose gambling addiction manifested early in their marriage. Within one month of marriage, Zelia was out of state with no money. She had funds wired to her so she could return home to visit her family. Within six months from that time, she accompanied Sherman to another state, with $200 wired by Big Mama for both of them to return home. During the ensuing ten-month period when Sherman and Zelia lived with Zelia's family, Dana Jane McClellan (my mother) was born. She arrived on May 19, 1925. Meanwhile, Sherman's restless attempts at establishing roots in Lynchburg were, on three separate occasions, funded by Zelia's family.

Sherman's profligate spending and his gambling addiction eventually resulted in the loss of Zelia's diamond ring, family land, and money needed by his young family. On August 7, 1930, after only six years of marriage, he "wilfully [sic] and without justification whatsoever, deserted and abandoned [Zelia] in the City of Asheville, North Carolina," leaving her and Dana penniless. Zelia also owed back board to a landlord in the amount of $97.

Several months before he walked out, Sherman wrote to his mother-in-law indicating his intention to pay back a loan from her in monthly installments of $100. Big Mama's repeated loans to him suggest that she always gave him the benefit of the doubt—or that she didn't want her daughter or granddaughter to suffer because of his irresponsibility. With no income and now a single parent, Zelia had no choice but to contact her oldest sister, Cora, for funds to travel to Farmville, Virginia. Once there, Zelia and Dana lived with Cora and her family.

Second Chances

Whether Sherman wanted a second chance from Zelia or not is unknown, but Zelia took a second chance at marriage on October 21, 1933. Less than three years after Sherman deserted her, she and Bascom Fennel Caufield, a widower from Pedlar Mills, Virginia, drove to Roxboro, North Carolina, and married at the Person County Courthouse.

Where or how they met remains a mystery. He was 30 years old, and she was 28. Bascom's first wife had died at the age of 28, leaving him with two children to raise, Homer and Phyllis. As best as I can tell, this was a marriage of convenience. Zelia thought she would attain financial security, and Bascom secured the mother for his young children that he needed.

My grandmother's view of men took shape early in her life in how she interpreted her own father's entrance into this world as an illegitimate child. At the turn of the century, this was a shameful family secret. Her view became further complicated by Sherman's addictions and subsequent abandonment. Adding insult to injury was an experience she documented as an employee of Dr. C. L. Morriss before her marriage to Bascom.

Here are sections of a letter Grandma wrote to her employer, long before the Me Too movement (spelling errors left intact):

> Dr. Morriss:
>
> I am sure that after the horrible experience of today you could not expect me to enter your office again. I do not know whether you were drunk or insane.
>
> I am sure that during my two years of hard and under pay I have never given you reason to think that I was anything but a lady. Had I thought you would have treated me otherwise I would have left long ago.
>
> Since you have made your diabolical and insulting proposition of today, certainly the vilest and crudest proposition a woman could possible be offered, and you have discovered that I am not the type that sells her womanhood and since you have so much money that you boasted that you could pay any amount for that type of pleasure then I feel sure that you can pay for the humiliating you made me past thru . . . I demand the sum of five hundred dollars. [Your proposal] leaves me without a job and my child to support for an indifinite time . . .
>
> Mrs. Zelia McClellan

The story does not end there for my grandmother or those of us who succeeded her. The way any family members deal with their beginnings affects those who come after them just as a stone thrown into a pond sends out concentric ripples. Those ripples can easily become waves crashing into the lives of those in the next generation if unresolved issues are not dealt with.

Whatever shame and secrecy my grandmother felt was surpassed by her inner strength, sacrifice, resolve, and resilience. She would not take the road of least resistance in any area of life. Just as Big Mama was generous in providing financial support when needed, my grandmother was generous in helping many people during her lifetime. I observed how she faced each day with determination, commitment, and hard work. Although she was very much a rule follower, she was committed to God, and her daily faith manifested itself in kindness and perseverance. Even in the face of adversity, she never complained.

How do experiences from former generations spill over into subsequent generations? Or, in unique cases, what keeps the pattern from being repeated? What happens? Where and how does God show up? Does He? Oh, yes, He does! And how He breaks the pattern is as unique as your thumbprint. He knows exactly what will reach the depths of your soul.

Unveiling a Spiritual Takeaway

The people in your family of origin have already experienced their share of life's ups and downs with their own beliefs about God, themselves, and others. If they are unable to share their personal stories, their emotional attachment to you will be diminished.

Unveiling Questions for Discussion

Entrance

- What is your backstory? [e.g. cultural climate at the time of your birth, current events, family of origin]
- What are your "ascribed" labels?
- Are these labels positive, negative, or neutral?
- Are you carrying an ascribed [negative] label into the present?
- Share how this label (positive, negative, neutral) affects you today.
- How has this negative label affected your ability to see yourself clearly?
- How has this label affected your role(s) as a woman?
- Has your family been veiled in a secret and/or shame?

Part II

WHO DO YOU SAY I AM?

Chapter Four

DAMAGED IDENTITY

But what about you? Who do you say that I am?

Matthew 16:15

The Thumbprint of Pain

Not long ago, I was catering a showroom at the High Point Furniture Market when I cut my thumb while opening a can of mandarin oranges. The security guard, who was also a fire and rescue responder, examined my thumb and quickly pointed out that the cut would change the way my thumbprint appeared. He commented that I would no longer be able to open my iPhone because the thumbprint that identified me had now changed.

In a spiritual sense, the pain and problems of life cut to the core of who we think we are, who others are, and who God is. These are the chapters of our present story that we did not ask for. This is when the story line—whether it results from our own failings and shortcomings or from others' actions—leads to what we see as negative consequences. Regardless of how our story begins, the plot thickens when life delivers unexpected outcomes. People are complicated, and story lines don't play out as we think they are supposed to. The sting of pain slashes the thumbprint of the life we imagined we would have. As a result of personal pain, our warped identity can manifest in unhealthy ways. We will compensate, and how! Hearts will attach to whatever and whomever they perceive will provide safety and security. Some will attach to God; others will attach to what they perceive will fill the God-shaped void in their hearts.

When unannounced, unplanned, and unsettling events interrupt our lives, the most critical question we can ask ourselves about how God views us is, "Who do you say that I am?" How we answer this question will be a direct reflection of our own self-image. Our answer will determine:

- Whether we walk in a damaged identity or the identity God has given us
- Whether we allow our experience to define us or walk confidently into the future
- Whether we think God is holding out on us or is also brokenhearted by what broke our heart (Psalm 34:18)

Here is how we learn to walk in a wrong identity:

Life > Loss > Loss Interpreted as a Lie > Label > Identity

How we interpret a loss of some kind will directly influence whether or not we are able to move forward from it. For some, we begin to believe a lie, which can either be about ourselves, others, or God. If a lie swirls around in our thoughts and perceptions for too long, then a negative label about ourselves—and possibly about God—begins to take root in our hearts and minds.

Self-Imposed Labels

The problem with psychological distress is that it insidiously knocks down the door of our heart and mind without our permission. Our value and worth evaporate while our thoughts become unwanted guests that wear out their welcome daily, if not hourly. And without ever questioning or challenging our tumultuous ways of perceiving what occurred, we readily label ourselves with negative descriptors.

Unfortunately for my mother and grandmother, their self-imposed labels took hold early. Grandma was a very young mother the day her husband walked out the door for the last time. For both Grandma and my mother, who was five years old when her daddy left, the labels stuck faster than the door could shut behind Sherman McClellan:

- "What did I do?"
- "I am unwanted. No one will ever want me."
- "I'm not good enough."
- "I don't deserve to be loved."
- "It's terrible to be deserted."
- "I am a failure."

I can imagine my grandmother wondered why God had seemingly abandoned her. To ask where God is during life's unexpected story lines is natural and justified. The problem comes when we assume the worst of our Creator. It can look like this:

- "God is distant in my life."
- "God doesn't care and is not involved in the details of my life."
- "I can't believe God would allow this to happen."
- "God is playing a cruel joke on me" or "God is punishing me."

If we allow the pain to become entangled with an incorrect concept of who God is, then our incorrect thinking will be followed by unhealthy or inappropriate ways of coping. Even if we allow what appear to be healthy ways of coping with disappointment, our spiritual journey will still be characterized by bondage to an untrue identity. I will refer to this as spiritual identity theft. Satan, the thief, is having the time of his life.

If we obsess on either end of the spectrum—focusing on good behaviors (e.g., going through the motions of religious practices) or bad behaviors (e.g., abusing drugs or alcohol, eating to meet emotional needs, or spending money excessively)—then we will be in spiritual bondage. Why? Because if you live a defeated life, Satan has won on this side of your eternal home. Take my word for it, that it is all he needs to keep you from reaching your destiny.

Then, without you even realizing it, wrong thinking has sidetracked the plan God had for your life (Jeremiah 29:11). As a result, you will walk through life with little confidence, damaged self-worth, and a sense that you have no value to those around you. And what results when pain is not dealt with correctly? You default to the deleterious behaviors to which you are naturally inclined.

Unveiling a Spiritual Takeaway

Our thoughts will default to a lie unless we have programmed our thinking with truth (John 17:15-17).

Chapter Five

IMAGE OF SELF: YOUR DNA DEFAULTS

Mom

My mother dealt with the pain of her absent father in the ways that came naturally to her. Known as a beautiful young lady by the time she was a young teen, her gregarious personality, combined with her attractiveness, made her popular with young men. By the age of 16, she defaulted to promiscuous behaviors to feel accepted and loved.

Although my grandmother remarried to fill the void my mother experienced when her father deserted the family, the relationship between my mother and her stepfather was not a close one. In fact, on July 12, 1941, two months after Mom's "Sweet 16" birthday, she wrote:

> I won't ever forget tonite . . . he [Bascom] nearly broke [Mom's] arm when she got in his way. I had a terrible heart spell after that but feel fine now— except that medicine makes me want to boo-hoo . . . He admitted something in a fit of temper I am going to tell you. He said, he married mums to keep from having a "shot gun" wedding with some McCraw gal. He knew the baby belonged to him. I hate him because he is more insane than responsible.

Clearly, my mother's views on men were strongly influenced by having been deserted by her own father and having seen her mother be poorly treated by both of her husbands. Dana escaped the problems of home with pleasantries of her social life. Her extroverted tendencies manifested in frequent telephone calls, girlfriends, movies, and boys. As her journals indicate, her favorite coping strategies involved boys.

From an emotional perspective, there was a lack of attachment to both her earthly father and her stepfather. Lacking a father figure and not being secure in the relationship with either man, she made up an idealized version of the father she dreamed of having. Later in Mom's life, she would tell people that her father was an American general. When I went through Mom's personal effects after she died, I found a photograph of a sign concerning Civil War general George McClellan. I suspect that between the name she shared with him and his prominence as a military leader, he represented an idealized version of whom she envisioned her father to be. Clearly, since George McClellan died in 1885, she did not claim that this particular person was her father, but it was important to her to promote a lofty image of her father as a means of impressing others. Coincidentally, her father, Sherman McClellan, shared not only his last name with a Civil War general, but his first name as well: George McClellan's subordinate William Sherman. But in Dana's life, the real Sherman might as well have been an imaginary figure, as he showed up only when it was convenient for him to do so.

Mom left for Longwood College, formerly known as State Teachers College, in the fall of 1943. Sherman's intermittent visits were sporadic and indefinite, and his lack of involvement and commitment would dog her for years to come.

In response to her father's abandonment, my mother defaulted to attention-getting behaviors and promiscuity. She finally got the attention from men that she had lacked in her life up to that point. Her pain eventually led her to embrace an incorrect and destructive identity that undermined her for decades.

Grandma

My grandmother was a wonderful woman. She remained devoted to Bascom, her second husband, even though she could have walked away from the marriage. He did not treasure her as he should have. Since she was not valued as she should have been by either husband, she defaulted in the way that came naturally to her and, in her mind, gave her worth: religious practices. From an early age, good behaviors trumped family secrets in her family of origin. She learned to cope with life's disappointments by doing good things. There's a fine line between commitment and legalism. In and of itself, church attendance is a good thing. For my grandmother, however, the unspoken rules for living were not a result of freedom, but of bondage. For example, when my parents and I returned stateside for good after my father's military retirement, I went to live with my grandmother which, coincidentally, happened just months after Bascom's death following two years of lung cancer. My grandmother laid down certain rules for the two of us to live by on Sundays:

- Do not wash clothes.
- Do not go to the movie theater.
- Do not shop.
- Do not play cards.

While Mom, as a young woman, defaulted to negative behaviors, Grandma defaulted to positive behaviors. Their unsettled hearts pursued a legitimate need we each have: to be loved and accepted. Mom thought attracting attention from young men would prove she was lovable, and Grandma labored under the erroneous assumption that she could earn God's love and approval by following legalistic rules and attending church gatherings as much as possible. Neither one was able to embrace God's unconditional love and grace because of what they had experienced through human relationships. Their identities never should have been defined by their life experiences to the extent that they were.

When loss is interpreted incorrectly as a negative label, you walk in a wrong identity. And the worst label of all? Victim. This is when you feel as though God has held out on you, making you question who you are and who He is. Even more, it is when you feel as though you have no mastery of the events of your life, and you perceive yourself to be an innocent bystander with an external locus of control. You simply watch as events unfold, questioning and doubting your choices. Remember the question, *Who do you say that I am?* For years I carried the label of "victim" and did not know it. The only difference between living as a victim and living as a victor is believing that God has remained distant in the details of your life. In my case, He chose to derail me by bringing me face to face with unresolved places of hurt. Why? Because He looked at my heart, not my going through the motions of everyday living which, by all appearances, included all the 'right' things. As He was with me, God is concerned about your heart, not your actions (I Samuel 16:7b).

Dad

My parents and I returned stateside to Arlington, Virginia, on December 15, 1964, two months after I turned two years old. My earliest memories are sometime before the age of four. At that time, we lived on the top floor of an apartment building. I recently visited that building and saw that it had been converted into a hotel. Snapshots within my memory still recall the hallway leading from the elevator to our apartment and our apartment windows that gave us a clear view of the Washington Monument. I vividly remember seeing my father crying in that hallway, and I even recall the shirt he was wearing. He was a resilient man except when it came to my mother's angry outbursts and verbal abuse.

My father's father, Dimitry Hirtzkoff, and his wife, Anna, originated from Galecia, Austria. Dimitry arrived at Ellis Island and worked in a Pittsburgh factory for a short time until he could go back to Austria to collect Anna and his three young children. Upon returning to the States, they settled in Bear Run, Minnesota, where seven more children were born, including my father in 1918. All ten siblings learned responsibility and hard work from a young age on the family farm. When the children reached high school age, they attended Hibbing High, a ten-mile walk from the farm. Sports and competitive games between siblings dominated my father's formative years. Dad's natural athleticism resulted in a football scholarship to the University of Minnesota. His mother, Anna, died in 1938 when he was only twenty years old. Loss began early for him and only continued as his college career was interrupted by World War II. Near the end of the war, on March 25, 1945, Dad's company lost more than 100 men while crossing the Rhine River. The commendation that accompanied Dad's Silver Star Medal reads as follows:

> *Captain Daniel Hritzko, 01110573, Corps of Engineers, 35th Engineer Combat Battalion, United States Army, for gallantry in action against the enemy on 25 March 1945, in Germany. Captain Hritzko's company had been given the mission of transporting an infantry battalion across the Rhine River in the face of determined enemy resistance. Throughout this hazardous operation from << H>> hour until the last boat-load of men and supplies had reached the opposite shore, Captain Hritzko was constantly in the open, exposed to the intense enemy fire, where he could apply his keen professional knowledge and superior leadership to the best advantage. His undaunted courage and galiant [sic] devotion to duty were an inspiration to all and in the finest tradition of the military service. Entered the military service from Minnesota.*

My mother said my father had told her that from that day forward, he would never get too close to anyone again. In Dad's personal effects, I found a letter from a mother in Arkansas whose son had died under Dad's command in World War II. From the letter, it is apparent that Dad had written to the family previously, and the mother replied asking for details about her son's last moments. I have no doubt that the horror and tragedy of war took a toll on Dad's mental health. In light of the understanding we have today, he may well have suffered from PTSD after serving in three wars and eight combat campaigns. While I can recall single events of Dad being engaged in my life, those moments were few and far between with the passage of time.

The Silver Star was one of many medals Dad received during his military career. He never mentioned or showed any of his medals to me. Like so many soldiers of the "greatest generation," he was a humble man, never asking for recognition of any kind. I discovered his medals before his death, tucked away in Band-aid boxes and stashed in drawers.

Mom: Looking for Love
While Dad was fighting in the war in March 1945, my mother, who had not returned to college in January of that same year, was working full-time and living with my grandmother and Bascom in Lynchburg. It would have been the spring semester of her sophomore year of college had she continued. In the prior year, while still attending State Teachers College in Farmville, Virginia, she had met Roland Byers, an army soldier, at a Camp Pickett mixer. He was temporarily stationed at the camp. Her diaries reflect an intense infatuation after their initial meeting, but with time, her emotions shifted toward the men who were available and present. Although Roland continued to write to her from Tokyo, Japan, she became enamored with the young man living next door. As indicated in her diary, she was "p." by this next door neighbor—undoubtedly her shorthand for "pregnant." She aborted the baby on February 10, as recorded in the last entry in her journal for the remainder of that year. She records that she was given a sulfa drug via a shot in her hip that "hurt like hell." Sulfa drugs were commonly given to women post-abortion during this era to prevent infection. Roland, whom she called Ronnie, returned two months later, and she married him on July 2, 1945, at First Baptist Church in Lynchburg.

Roland's military assignments took the newlyweds to Ft. Bragg, North Carolina; Ft. Hood, Texas; and eventually back to Tokyo. Roland traveled to Japan ahead of Mom. With Roland gone, her restless heart began to wander, crave, and yearn.

Even while my mother was en route to Japan to reunite with Roland, she wrote to another man declaring her love and devotion to him, not to her husband. Years later, while I was a freshman in college in the early 1980s, this man and my mother somehow got reacquainted even though she was still married to my father. He sent her copies of letters she had sent to him during the war, hoping to rekindle the affair that had started while Mom and Roland were courting. I learned in recent years that this man had served a two-year prison sentence for the involuntary manslaughter of his wife in a drunken rage in 1969. At the time of this writing, his grown son resides in Atlanta, Georgia, where he represents high-profile clients as a criminal defense attorney.

Meanwhile, across the globe, Dad married a French woman on March 16, 1946. They had one daughter and moved to Toledo, Ohio, where Dad completed his undergraduate degree. The marriage was short-lived, however, and it is my understanding that his wife was homesick for France. She returned there with their daughter, and the couple later divorced.

Dad continued with his military career, including deployments to South Korea, the Panama Canal Zone, and eventually to Arlington. Mom's divorce decree stated that she "abandoned" Roland in 1957, repeating what her father had done to her. She went on to reside in Greensboro, North Carolina; Roanoke, Virginia; and eventually Washington, DC, where she met my father in December 1960. Between 1957 and 1960, a handful of unfortunate men were caught in the wake of her shifting affections and eventual abandonment.

Military Life
After our departure from Arlington in the mid-1960s and subsequent military assignment in Stuttgart, Germany, Dad's career took him to

Vietnam. Mom and I traveled frequently between Lynchburg and Stuttgart. I began my kindergarten year at Lynchburg Christian Academy in 1967, the year of the school's inception. While back-and-forth travel during kindergarten and first grades made for a disjointed academic start, we were settled in Stuttgart for all of my second grade year. I have fond memories of living at Patch Barracks in Stuttgart. Mom rode our school bus on cold days handing out treat bags to children attending the American school. Carefree afternoons were spent with other military children playing outside on the massive lawns separating military housing. My best friend, Lynne, often accompanied my family and me on vacations throughout Europe. During my second grade year, I attended school for no more than a total of two months. According to Mom, my teacher believed that traveling provided a better education than sitting in the classroom. On the days we weren't traveling, Dad would leave for work in full military attire before I left for school. I thought he was the most handsome man I had ever seen.

Dad's sporadic absences during the Vietnam War created opportunities for Mom's restless heart to wander, a pattern that continued throughout their forty-year marriage. I recall traveling to places so Mom could visit with men who were not my father, as I had no choice but to go along. By the summer of 1971, we moved back to Lynchburg permanently. As I think back on my years in middle and high school in the 1970s, I can recall Mom's flirtatious and histrionic tendencies toward wealthy businessmen in Lynchburg. Even though I was living with my grandmother during this time, I was quite aware of my mother's actions. My father, who left active military service in 1971, returned to his passion of teaching and coaching at a new school in nearby Forest, Virginia. He devoted endless hours as a head football coach and teacher. His love of sports was the outlet and escape he needed from his trying marriage. During this period, Mom worked in the fields of communication and human resources, with much of her work involving employing people for temporary jobs in Lynchburg.

Living with Grandma

People who knew me in Lynchburg often wondered why I lived with my grandmother when my parents also resided in Lynchburg. The overarching explanation is that my grandmother was able to provide the stability I needed as a child. But there were multiple reasons for this arrangement. First, our decision to return to Lynchburg happened as my third-grade year was about to begin. My parents needed to tie up their military loose ends in Arlington before they could reside permanently in Lynchburg, so it made sense for me to move in with my grandmother to start the school year.

Second, my grandmother's second husband had just passed away after a grueling battle with lung cancer, so she was glad to have my company and was in a position to care for me. Also, her home was located close to my school and to our church, so I was able to get to where I needed to go since she had no car.

Third, and perhaps most significantly, my mother did not want the responsibility of motherhood. Her gregarious and extroverted nature craved attention and acceptance in social circles. Because of this, the daily routine of motherhood would have been too mundane. And finally, by that time, my father's alcoholism was already an issue infiltrating his life beyond the home. I recall being at a nearby church camp one summer in middle school and meeting a male student who attended the school where Dad taught. He informed me that he knew Coach Hritzko "drank vodka in the supply closet" during the day.

Another unfortunate episode was told to Grandma and me when Mom called one night informing us that the police had picked up Dad in downtown Lynchburg while he was inebriated. From ages eight to seventeen, I spent Friday nights with my parents at their house on Langhorne Road, sometimes walking next door to hear a teenage girl who was six years older than I was play and sing at the piano.

Caught in the Middle

My happy moments of growing up—listening to ABBA albums, shopping with my best friend on Saturdays at nearby Pitman Plaza, and spending time with a neighborhood girlfriend—were always interspersed with tumultuous Friday nights at my parents' house. These typically featured Dad drinking while preparing dinner, and Mom yelling for hours on end. My happiest times revolved around my involvement in my church's youth group, which included singing in the choir, playing handbells, and spending summer weeks at Eagle Eyrie, Virginia. Sometimes my emotional scale was tipped in favor of moments that provided security and stability, and other times it swung the opposite direction when my parents' conflicts brought on insecurity and instability. My worst recollections are from a Friday night when Mom and Dad argued all night, resulting in Dad falling down the basement stairs and Mom throwing furniture at him. I did not sleep at all that night, instead laying in a fetal position on the basement sectional while cigarette butts covered the coffee table alongside *Playboy* and *Playgirl* magazines and books about Janis Joplin. This night, as on many others, I would ask myself this question: "Why did God give me these parents?"

On the days I lived with my grandmother, we would sometimes sit together and cry on my bed. She was well aware of the turbulence of my parents' marriage. Life with her provided the stability that any child or teenager would want. Nonetheless, there was a significant generation gap between us, so there were many times that I closed up and did not share my true feelings with her. Shutting down and stuffing my emotions became a way for me to deal with my parents' painful lifestyle choices. Whereas my mother had externalized her pain and acted out at my age, I learned to cope at the opposite end of the spectrum by internalizing my feelings about the things or people who disappointed me.

I had made a profession of faith after my sixth grade year, but my value and worth—my spiritual DNA default—was found in making good grades and being as good of a child as my mother had been a bad one. My heart attached to these aspects of performance that seemed to provide me with worth and value.

First Crush

When I was an eighth-grade girl, my mother and I had only one thing in common: shopping. On a fall day at the start of eighth grade, we were shopping at Pitman Plaza when we encountered a college freshman (a young man) who was earning money while attending college in Lynchburg. I had an immediate crush on this older guy. Two years later, he asked me out on a double date, only to be embarrassed when the other couple learned I was a high school student while the four of us ate at a local restaurant during our double date.

My crush on this young man continued even after he graduated from college and returned to his hometown. Then, when I was a junior in high school, I was devastated to learn of his marriage to a girl from his hometown. My grandmother's unsuccessful attempts to console me carried over into the remainder of that year and into my senior year. My middle school infatuation had blossomed into a teenage crush that was based on just enough information about him to keep me fascinated about what I perceived to be a perfect guy. I began to make sweeping assumptions about him, although not based on much fact or truth. And when you have no idea of what a healthy marriage looks like, you create your own fantasy for what you think it should look like and who the handsome prince is to be. I was painfully shy, lacked confidence, and had little self-worth while growing up. These things prevented me from getting to know him very well. Eerily, my infatuation resembled my mother's idealistic perception of who she wanted her father to be. Unfortunately, my formative years did not involve any guidance from my father regarding issues concerning young men. In addition, I had no role modeling of what a healthy relationship was to look like between the opposite sexes.

College Years and Marriage

By the time I entered college, my father continued to work as a teacher and coach, but he had checked out emotionally. On my first visit home from college after having been away for about eight weeks, he was too inebriated to see me. Mom never covered for my father, nor did she give an explanation for this behavior even though my visit home had been planned since before my departure for college. My immediate thought was, "I'm not worthy enough for him to see me on my first visit home." It sent a message that I didn't matter as much as the bottle that had become an easy escape for him.

My husband and I became engaged a month shy of our graduation from Wake Forest University. I spent the summer of 1984 working a part-time job to earn money for honeymoon clothes and purchase a handful of Christmas presents. Tension rose between my mother and me as I tried unsuccessfully to enlist her assistance in wedding planning. My grandmother took me shopping for my wedding gown and peignoir set, taking great pride in purchasing both on her limited income.

On an August day, a couple of weeks before I started paralegal school in Atlanta, I drove my grandmother to Fort Hill Village Shopping Center to grocery shop. While Grandma was shopping, I visited another store in the strip mall. As I walked back to my parked car, an elderly man hit me. I was walking at a slant and did not see his approaching vehicle. Because of my height, I was propelled onto his hood instead of being knocked down under the car. My last memory was watching my Bass Weejun sandal fly through the air against the summer blue sky thinking, "This is it. Today I go to heaven." I closed my eyes, became unconscious, and rolled off the car onto the pavement. The ambulance arrived and transported me to a local hospital for examination. Thankfully, my only permanent physical injury wasn't life-threatening or extremely problematic. The legal aspects of the case could not be settled out of court, so Grandma accompanied me to court in the spring of 1986, nearly two years later. The attorney who represented me became well acquainted with my grandmother and me during this period of time. Little did I realize that God was preparing me for what was yet to come.

Have you ever had what you thought was a near-death experience? Did your perspective on life change after the event? If so, how?

Dad retired several months before my marriage in December 1984. My husband and I were newlyweds while he attended dental school and I worked to support us. Unfortunately, my mother opposed the marriage, for reasons I explain below. Two weeks after we were married, I was at work at the law firm in Durham, North Carolina, where I was a paralegal. I received a telephone call from a private investigator. He wanted to know why I had stopped making payments on my car. Further inquiry gave way to clarity. My mother had forged my name on a bank note to purchase the car my father drove. She stopped making payments, and the bank had hired a private investigator to find me. After telling this man on the phone that my mother was best friends with the vice president of the bank and that he might want to look into the origin of the bank note, I was never contacted again.

Grandma Takes III
In March 1987, I returned to our apartment one evening. My husband had the unfortunate task of telling me that my grandmother had had a massive stroke. She died six weeks later, on April 20, after having been rendered unable to speak and being paralyzed on one side. I was in shock at how the events of her life changed in one morning. My father had taken her to the doctor for an annual exam. He had pulled up in front of her house to drop her off, but when he asked her a question, he got no response. He knew something was wrong and called the ambulance, which transported her to the hospital. How does someone have a stroke right after leaving a doctor's appointment?

The one person in my life who had provided stability was gone. I wish I had told her how I felt about her during the days preceding her death, even though she would have been unable to respond. When she died, my emotions were ambivalent. On the one hand, I could not fully grasp that she was gone. For sure, I was in denial. On the other, my husband and I were establishing our new family of two and, because of all of the pushback we received from my mother prior to our marriage, I found myself pulling away from every member of my family of origin. This was unfair to my grandmother, who was emotionally supportive. My actions, however, manifested in the form of pulling away from everyone. I was going to show them all that we could do this, and I would never ask for a dime, even though our gross annual income was actually at the poverty level. It was unfair that I didn't attach emotionally to my grandmother during this time, or even as she lay on her deathbed. That is a regret I will always have. I did not truly appreciate the impact she had on my life until years later.

With Grandma gone, my relationship with my parents remained quite superficial. Dad's alcoholism made him emotionally distant and generally unable to engage in my life. As usual, things were more complicated with my mother. I was grappling with hard feelings resulting from her having intentionally contacted my college friends during my engagement to have them talk me out of marriage. My husband is a wonderful, caring man who is respected by all who know him, but in my mother's flawed thinking about the men in her childhood, she was certain he was going to use me to support him through dental school and then dump me. Nothing could have been further from the truth. With all this drama going on, I focused on my husband's last year in dental school, my job in Durham, and dealing with the stress I felt as the sole provider for my husband and me.

Broken Trust
My husband and I moved to High Point, North Carolina, in July 1988, so he could begin his private practice. The following year, I learned from my mother that the insurance on Grandma's house (where I grew up) had lapsed. Compelled to retrieve my personal belongings, I rented a

U-Haul truck and took several days off from work. On a summer night at the house with my parents present, I discovered my grandmother's holographic will and other important papers in a box in the dining room. When I told Mom I had discovered Grandma's will, she immediately snatched it from my hand, at which time I convinced her to let me read it out loud since neither she nor Dad had their glasses. The will indicated that Grandma had left everything to me except for one marble-top table. My mother grabbed the will out of my hand and ran out of the house. My father remained silent and sat quietly while watching these events unfold before him. Later, I was able to tape record a conversation with my mother that included her admitting to the will and its contents. She remained indignant and distant in the days I was in Lynchburg that week to gather my belongings.

Unfortunately, in the weeks that followed, my mother did more than just feel indignant about being left out of my grandmother's will; she destroyed the will itself. Then, Mom told me that the house had been sold and even gave me a fictitious name of the lawyer who supposedly handled the closing. As fate would have it, I already had a strong connection with the attorney who had represented me in my physical injury lawsuit. My lawyer's paralegal ran to the courthouse on the very day Mom told me she had sold Grandma's house. She skillfully intercepted the deed before the sale could be executed, and then her boss had the funds frozen to prevent their disbursement to Mom. As a result of Mom's anger over being thwarted and my hurt over being cheated, Mom and I did not talk for almost nine months. Dad never called me during that period.

Breaking Through with Dad

The years following this ordeal were unsettling for me emotionally. Every visit to Lynchburg was obligatory on my behalf. The weekend of September 13, 1996, was no different except for events that occurred on Sunday. Mom and Dad joined my husband (Joel), our sons, and me at the church where Grandma and I had been members. The pastor had been on vacation for the two weeks prior, and this was his first week back in the pulpit. I cannot tell you what the sermon content was about, but I sat rigidly on the pew feeling convicted by the Holy Spirit to speak to my father that day about his spiritual standing. I had never felt convicted as deeply as I did that day. I knew that before we returned home to North Carolina, I was compelled to talk to Dad.

After the service, we all met for lunch at a downtown hotel known for its Sunday buffet. The six of us followed our normal routine. Joel and Dad kept the conversation on sports. Mom carried on about different topics that never went beyond a level of superficiality. My father habituated to the same routine that he had always followed when eating at my grandmother's house. He ate, rose from the table, and waited elsewhere while everyone else finished their meal. I thought I had missed my opportunity to speak to him. How was I going to speak to him? What was I going to say?

Meanwhile, Joel and the boys returned to our hotel room to pack our bags. As they left, the Rev. Jerry Falwell and his entourage arrived. I had known Dr. Falwell my entire life, so he politely stopped, spoke, and proceeded to his lunch table. Then Dad did the unthinkable. He returned to the table. I knew this was my chance. To this day, evangelism is not one of my spiritual gifts, but I simply asked if he understood what the preacher had spoken from the pulpit. He said he did not, so in my very inexperienced and awkward way, I tried to simply explain what was said. He seemed interested in my explanation. Mom was indignant about my efforts to talk to Dad, and she showed her annoyance on her face, accompanied by an equally irritated tone. "He was raised Ukrainian, you know, Shirene." I had to sternly tell her to stop interrupting my conversation with him. When I finally came to a stopping point, Dad showed interest in what I had shared. I excused myself to the hotel room, where Joel wondered if I had coerced Jerry to speak to my dad. My response was that the Holy Spirit had convicted me to talk to Dad, not to have Dr. Falwell do so. Upon returning to the hotel lobby where my parents waited for us, I felt compelled to summarize our earlier conversation and to have Joel share a few words with Dad. I left Lynchburg that day knowing that Dad had been changed. I was even more surprised to find out that in the following week, he and Mom and gone back to my church, where he walked the aisle to make his decision public.

Dad's public profession of faith was nothing short of a miracle taking place before my eyes. Have you ever felt like anyone in your life is beyond the reach of God? Have you seen God show up in unexpected and miraculous ways?

The Trials of Caregiving

In the mid-1990s following the births of my sons, I began a period of caregiving as my parents' health declined. Honestly, I was resentful. As their only child, I felt obligated to help them, but after the way my upbringing had gone and how I had been treated as an adult, I was less than enthusiastic about bearing this burden. Early into caregiving, I discovered, as their respective power of attorney, that my mother had arranged for my father's federal tax liens to be put in his name, thereby absolving her of any financial responsibility. I have no idea whether he was aware of this or not. What would have been a sizable monthly military pension was being garnished by the Internal Revenue Service. The amount he owed in back taxes had reached six figures. The reason for not filing federal income taxes may have been that my father (incorrectly) believed Mom was taking care of it. It may also have been just a symptom of his depression and emotional detachment from life several years after his military retirement. Mom's spending addiction trumped financial responsibilities of any kind. Judgments and liens were numerous against both of them when I researched the public records. While they were still living in their apartment, I recall visiting one day when I noticed stacks of statements on the bar near the door. When I inquired about why these bills had not been opened, Mom's reply was, "I don't have to open [the bills] if there isn't money to pay them."

One time I had to intercept money from the estate of Dad's sister. My aunt had died intestate, thereby making Dad one of her heirs. If I had not done so, Mom would have spent every cent, as she had done with the early disbursements of estate funds. I also managed Dad's medical care with the help of his doctors at the VA hospital in Salem, Virginia. Dad's vascular dementia would come and go. Some days he recognized me; on other days he did not. Following the advice of my North Carolina attorney, I arranged for my father's care without telling my mother what I was doing on his behalf.

I had an epiphany about Dad on a cold winter day in 1999 as I drove him to an appointment in Salem. He was staring out the car window, bundled up in his winter coat. In that very moment, God gave me a complete peace for who my dad had and had not been. I believe that that peace was the impetus for me to act on behalf of my father from that day forward. Where he had worked tirelessly on my behalf when I was an infant to get me out of Iran, now the tables were turned. I was working tirelessly on his behalf without him knowing any of the complicated details. Did he know of the financial and legal problems that had now swallowed up his life? I'll never know.

Many times, others' irresponsibilities, addictions, and poor choices affect our lives. Has this been your experience? If so, what was your reaction? How have you seen God work through such situations?

I was able to get Dad's federal tax lien released so he could eventually afford to live at a facility in Forest, Virginia. There, he was a short car ride from my mother's apartment. I had taken care of the placement and discharge from the VA in an effort for them to at least see each other when a neighbor could drive Mom. She was furious that he had come home to the Lynchburg area. Her belief was that the VA Medical Center should take care of him since his military service for over three decades was payment for his care. In a telephone call several months prior, I had told her I was working to bring him back to the Lynchburg area, as he could not stay indefinitely at the VA hospital. She indicated she didn't want him back home because he wasn't the man she had married. It was the one time I screamed at her and said, "You're not the same woman he married. I've been to hell and back for the two of you." Now I was furious. She had no idea of what I was trying to do on behalf of each of them. I felt bitter for having to take care of an almost twenty-year financial problem that infiltrated every detail of their lives and limited the available options in their older years.

While all this was going on with my father, my mother was doing poorly, too. Her anger and emotional outbursts only got worse with the onset of Alzheimer's. Her disease manifested mainly in the form of short-term memory loss. She could not remember from month to month that I had taken over payment of her monthly bills. Repeatedly, she would call and verbally abuse me, as now I was the only available target. My communications with her doctor in Lynchburg were limited, as he would not talk with me when she threatened him about doing so. Although he knew the issues at hand and that I was her power of attorney, he refused to talk to me or give me results of tests when she had targeted him with her outbursts. Regardless of the doctor's overt rudeness and lack of empathy, I do believe God granted me strength to be my mother's advocate. The peace that passes all understanding became the bedrock under my daily doses of proactivity and pain. I was trying to do what was true, noble, right, pure, lovely, and admirable as my mother's caregiver despite how she had treated me for years.

What occurs deep within your soul when you are mistreated? What emotions are sparked? Do you handle it positively or negatively? What do you learn about yourself and others in these difficult situations?

A turning point came when she suffered a broken hip after her swollen legs got tangled in her dog's leash and she fell. She never returned home again. In the months that followed, I made solo trips to Lynchburg to clean out my parents' apartment. I had to go through all their possessions. There were many nights when I slept restlessly for a few hours while surrounded by stacks of magazines, unopened mail and bills, clothes, and dirty dishes. The task was lonely and emotionally overwhelming. Included in my mother's personal effects were things such as Polaroid photos taken by lovers that had not been thrown away. As my heart grew fonder of my father, it grew more distant and angry at my mother. While cleaning out their apartment, I had decided to move my father near me in North Carolina if my mother passed first. My visits to assisted living facilities had yielded positive outcomes, and I felt good about the plan I had in place.

Sudden Loss
On July 23, 2001, the day of the city swim meet for my sons, I packed our bags for everything we needed for the day. The one thing I forgot to take was my cell phone. Not long into the competition, I looked up to see my husband and father-in-law, who had come to inform me that I needed to pack an overnight bag and hurry to Lynchburg. I was overcome by my sense that my father had passed, which my husband confirmed when I asked him directly. My father had died unexpectedly while in the emergency room at Lynchburg General Hospital.

My emotions could not catch up to the facts, it seemed. I did not realize until after he had passed that the emergency room doctor had been on the telephone on and off with my husband all morning regarding my father's admission and the unsuccessful attempts to stabilize his condition. I should have been the one to be at the hospital or, at the very least, to have been in conversation with the doctor on call. I grieved with regret for not being with my father; in fact, no one was with him when he died. To this day, I don't even know what prompted the assisted living facility to call for an ambulance. There were too many details occurring between the two of my parents for me to get a handle on every aspect.

At the moment of Dad's death, my mother was on the cardiac floor of the same hospital being treated for an irregular heartbeat. I buried my father at Arlington National Cemetery three weeks later without telling her. I delivered the eulogy and accepted the flag in her place. My only regret was not walking behind the caisson in the sweltering heat on that August day. I should have walked to honor the man who went to great lengths to adopt me. I should have walked as a sign of respect for the leader he was to hundreds of men. I should have walked tall for him because, in his last years, he was made small. For all his failings as a parent, I still loved him and felt he deserved my respect for his exemplary service to our country. As I laid Dad to rest, I found myself quite mad at God. He had taken the easy parent from me when I had planned everything out. Dad was going to live with me in North Carolina, where I could regularly visit him in a memory care facility. I never got to have that sweet time with him away from the toxic influence of my mother.

Have you ever had a life experience when you believed that "it wasn't supposed to be this way?" Were your beliefs changed for the better or for the worse?

In the weeks following my father's death, my mother's body faltered and failed. Although I had already told her about Dad's death on the day of his passing, I had to make the tough decision to not even share the details of his burial at Arlington. There was no conceivable way to transport her for the ceremony. By the time of Dad's death, Mom had had two hip replacements, only to have the first hip dislocate and require surgery the week after his burial. It was during this hospital stay that she asked if I had seen my father recently. When I answered, "No, I haven't seen him lately," she looked at me and curiously asked if he had died. Upon hearing the truth, it was if she had heard it for the first time.

She seemed surprised at this news. Her short-term memory had not recalled the event of his death from several weeks prior.

My mother recuperated from her hip surgery at Guggenheimer Nursing Home in Lynchburg. Ironically, she was in the same facility where her grandmother, Big Mama, had died many years earlier from a broken hip. Now, history was repeating itself two generations later.

Unexpected Grace

I drove spontaneously to Lynchburg for the day on September 21, 2001, to visit Mom. My car visits in the months after Dad's death were unplanned and spur-of-the-moment, depending on the need or crisis of the day. With two young children at home, I did not have the liberty to be with her at all times. Just twenty-four hours after my September 21 visit, Mom's doctor called to inform me of her rising temperature and swelling. In addition to her hip issues, she was suffering from collapsed veins. Without any pushback, my husband agreed that I needed to go to Lynchburg to be with her.

What I found when I entered room 215 was a woman who was more lucid than she had been in two years. She was already deep in thought. When her eyes looked at me, her first comment was, "You don't deserve this." Although I told her it was alright, in reality, I couldn't have agreed with her more. As I looked at her lying under the covers on her bed, the only thing worse than her impending death was the blanket of superficiality that had covered our relationship the preceding 20 years. In a sense, I was dying too. My mental checklist of what I didn't deserve had been written one page at a time for many years. I could have walked away from the relationship on a number of occasions and been justified in doing so, especially as an adult with a life of my own. But I kept going back, many times not knowing why. Mostly I went out of obligation as an only child. I was weary, troubled, angry, and even more upset that God had left me with the difficult parent.

Now, as the last chapter approached, the ink seemed indelible. And here I was, once again, with regrets of my own. Regrets that an ideal mother-daughter relationship would never be mine. My feelings had only been complicated with the onset of Alzheimer's affecting her short-term memory. There were many times during the last few years that my life would have been much easier if she *hadn't* recognized me. But now, as I sat by her bedside, her recognition became God's gift. There she lay, a woman, near death, who was completely burdened by the life she had lived and the choices she had made. She could no longer run from the hurt within her own heart. I needn't be her judge. Her life had been her judgment. I could see it in her eyes. I took her shriveled hands—something I hadn't done in years—and in the sacred stillness of the room, the veils of hurt, unkind words, and misunderstanding were torn as she was drawn to Christ. At my initiation, I remember telling her how to pray for forgiveness and asking God to touch her heart. I don't know what God told her after she prayed, but with her eyes closed with peace replacing burden, all she could say was "Thank you, Jesus." She had been touched by grace and would never be the same. I beheld God's glory in her life that night. But sometimes that's where you behold His glory—in the places you least expect to find it. She died six days later.

Have you had a life event occur that completely dissolved your anger or bitterness because God showed up in a powerful way?

My mother's passing ushered in round two of writing an obituary, delivering a eulogy, and shaking hands with those who came to pay respects. I would discover in the days immediately following Mom's death that she had never finished college. My suspicion arose when I noticed that several versions of her resume contained conflicting facts. I called her favorite cousin to inquire, and the cousin confirmed that the resumes embellished Mom's education. Once again, lies were unveiled and truth was revealed. But I did not have time to process another lie. Rather, making funeral arrangements with the funeral home and church where I grew up demanded my full attention. People from my mother's past showed up for the service. One friend indicated that my mother had given her a peace lily in 1989 that had never bloomed until the day of my mother's passing. I believe this story was God's way of showing up in the smallest of details to give me reassurance that Mom's heart and soul were finally at rest.

Stress Takes Its Toll

In many ways, there was no one in my life who could relate to me emotionally, as none of my friends had had parents who had passed. I recall climbing my basement steps wondering if I would ever laugh again. With two deaths and two funerals in eight weeks, stress had clearly taken its toll on me in numerous ways. I was depleted and wiped out. Stress can infiltrate every compartment of life: spiritual, relational, emotional, and physical. I would like to say that my husband and I were on the same proverbial page while I was caregiving, but we weren't. We drifted apart emotionally because of my frequent absence and his protective nature when I would spend yet another day on the road. Months after Mom passed, he shared that he had not wanted me to visit her due to her volatile emotional state, as he was concerned for my safety. He had seen enough to know what she was capable of. Had I known this at the time, I would have understood him pushing back about my travel. When I was in the thick of caregiving, he would make comments asserting that the state should take care of her, not me. He carried a huge load in managing his growing dental practice and tending to our sons if I hadn't returned by evening. Emotionally, I became distant from him because I felt he didn't understand what I was going through as my parents' only child. He saw that caregiving was taking its toll on me and us.

The cumulative effects of stress became evident in my short-term memory. Details that I would normally have no trouble managing seemed overwhelming. It was all I could do to go through the motions of daily living. In spite of feeling at loose ends, I actually functioned quite well, or so I thought. Inwardly, my thought life was a mess, but outwardly, I continued to do the "right" things: lead Bible studies, serve as a deacon's helpful wife, and care for my children. The only outlet I had for self-care was exercising, which, at times, became obsessive.

The Healing Begins

And then, a spiritual milestone occurred. On my mother's birthday just months after her death, I went to church alone while my husband attended a dental convention. The guest pastor had a wonderful sermon, and at the close of the hour, I made my way to the altar to pray, "Lord, I'll do whatever it takes to have an impact for you." What I meant by this prayer was for God to make a way for me to share my mother's deathbed conversion. Instead, God used it as an invitation to correct my victim identity once and for all. How did He do it? By touching the deepest place of hurt in a teenage girl's heart. In less than 48 hours after praying this prayer, I received a telephone call from the college boy who had broken my heart. His second wife had recently left their marriage, and he was testing the waters by offering me the bait of temptation. He had located me through my father's online obituary and then a subsequent call to directory assistance. What should have meant nothing to me made me stop in my tracks.

This out-of-the-blue telephone call came as a total surprise. Now, all of these years later, he called *me*, not the other way around. Not only that, he had kept photographs taken at the beach when he and his brother visited me on a trip with my best friend and my mother. His comments took me back to my 16-year-old broken heart. I felt compelled to share about my mother's deathbed conversion, but he wasn't interested. He was interested in only one thing. Somehow, I had the presence of mind to say that it was nice to hear from him, while making it clear—if only indirectly—that my loyalty to my marriage and family was unwavering. He ended the telephone call abruptly when he realized I wasn't going to take the bait. I never heard from him again. This is how God dealt with the unhealed place in my heart. He took me right back to it while, at the same time, allowing Satan to use temptation! God knew what I didn't:

that in order to heal me from the inside out, He would have to take me to the place of pain.

In Beth Moore's book *When Godly People Do Ungodly Things*, she references the spiritual sifting that needed to take place in Peter before he could make a spiritual impact on others' lives. As she words it, "Satan had a sieve. Christ had a purpose. The two collided." (p. 92)

I believe in spiritual realms where we have no inkling of what goes on or what is at stake. Now that I look back on these events, I believe Satan asked God for permission to test me. At the time, however, there was only one thing I knew as I was struggling: Satan desperately longed for my downfall. I therefore surmised that I must be a threat or else he would not have gone to such lengths to trap me. At that point, I had no awareness that I needed to change my thinking or even that I could. As far as I knew, thoughts were just thoughts—unchallenged and always true.

Has God ever used an event in your life to get your attention? I wonder if, as He did for me, He is prompting your heart for you to start walking in the identity that He intends for you.

God knew what the months ahead would mean for me: learning to make some exchanges in my thinking, changing my perceptions of myself, and recognizing God's sovereignty in every detail of my life. And the only way He could do that was to bring me face to face with the unresolved hurt that had been interpreted incorrectly ("I'm not worthy enough"). This deep hurt caused me to second-guess my own decisions ("Did I marry the right person?") and live in doubt ("If I had had a different upbringing, would I have made different choices?").

Gaining Victory Over Feelings
On my worst days, I was convinced that my life was of no worth or value. As I reflect on the depressive state that overwhelmed me, I recall

thinking that my life's purpose was only to birth two sons. I thought my husband should have married someone else, and that he deserved a better spouse. I believed I had messed up everyone's life in my immediate family. There were days when sleep was my only escape from the downward spiral that was my thought life. I covered my anguish well, as even those closest to me did not know about the internal struggle I was undergoing. But those deepest and darkest days, agonizing as they were, were the beginning of a transformed life that I refer to as "being born again again."

During those days, I poured over Scripture as I never had before. I learned so much about God during that time. 2 Samuel 7:18–29 became the passage that God used to show me His sovereignty. God does not delight in events that hurt us. But we must learn to separate *who* He is from *what* He allows to occur in our lives. The words "O Sovereign Lord" appear seven times in this 2 Samuel passage. When confronting pain, hurt, and loss, we should admit the loss and its effects on our hearts. But the heart and mind are directly related. In fact, the Hebrew word in the Old Testament used for *heart* is the same word used for *mind*. If we learn to think incorrectly about truth, then our feelings will deceive us (Jeremiah 17:9). Our feelings are not always reliable, especially when it comes to knowing truth (though they often reveal what we think about something). The brain is more than capable of being renewed and changed (Romans 12:1, 2). There is even a scientific term for this ability to adapt: *neuroplasticity*.

The challenge in sizing up the truth is that the stories we tell ourselves do not get fact checked. We just believe them to be true. And when we do not fact check our personal narratives, we inevitably default to what we think works best for us. Here is a quick synopsis on how the women in my family dealt with life's disappointments: my grandmother internalized her pain by spiritualizing her behaviors, my mother soothed her pain by running into the arms of others, and I dealt with my disappointments by stuffing my emotions.

Other options that people resort to include substance use/abuse, eating, spending, and pursuing achievements. These responses can be what a person uses to either ignore negative emotions and gain a quick, temporary fix, or to affirm personal worth (grades, financial status, workaholism).

The way to triumph over our false personal narratives is to pay attention to what we are telling ourselves. Then, we must replace lies with truth in our thinking. Are you ready? Let's begin!

Unveiling a Spiritual Takeaway

If emotional attachment in your family of origin has been compromised, your heart will attach to what seems to work—overeating, overspending, fixating on performance, acting inappropriately sexually, being a workaholic, and/or engaging in other addictions. While some people naturally attach their hearts to God because they have a healthy view of who He is—a safe and secure provision during challenging times—people who do not naturally cling to God in their pain may potentially turn to quick fixes and unhealthy behaviors to fill the void.

Chapter Six

CHANGE YOUR STORY

You are not a pawn, a victim of circumstances beyond your control.

Instead, you are responsible for your own life.

No one else can take your turn.

John Ortberg,

When the Game Is Over It All Goes Back in the Box

God loves you so much that He is willing to do whatever it takes for you to start walking in the identity and destiny He has for you. For me, He did this by touching the parts of my heart I didn't want to even acknowledge, much less surrender. When we hold on to those places of disappointment, hurt, and loss we are walking through life as a pawn. God wants so much more for you! Since He has created each of us with dominion and volition, that requires change and hard work.

For our personal narratives to change, we have to change our story line. We need to look at generational patterns (usually going back for three generations) to see what strongholds need to be broken. In so doing, we will fact check the stories we tell ourselves about God, life, and who we are. If this sounds like a worthwhile and beneficial endeavor to you, know that it will require diligent, determined effort on your part. In the event that you recognize a generational pattern, consider yourself a member of what I call the "pivotal generation." That means you can be the person who does the hard, internal work of preventing a dysfunctional family pattern from continuing. In my family, specifically, the pattern of unhealthy—even toxic—marriages needed to stop with me. To succeed in breaking this pattern, I had to make mental exchanges that worked for my good—maritally, spiritually, and emotionally. Revamping the way I thought about myself and my family history also helped me to become a more effective, healthy parent to my sons. Just as none of us gets to choose our DNA, I had no say about the family into which I was adopted. But this, too, was orchestrated by God so I could understand the higher concepts of sovereignty, redemption, purpose, and what it is truly like to become a new creation.

Exchanges

If you are ready to make headway in understanding who you are in Christ, start thinking about Christ's crucifixion in a new way. Rather than just believing it is the event that we celebrate at Easter, think about this "glorious exchange" as it applies to your life along with its implications for victorious living.

A recent trip for blood work gave way to this thought: "I wonder what imperfections will show up in my blood?" As God often does with me, this analogy provided a spiritual truth tied to Christ's death: He took on every imperfect act, sin, or pain that this world could send our way—big, small, and anything in between. Christ received unto himself *any* and *every* act that would affect our hearts. The problem is that we won't let these things die in our hearts or minds, because we still hold incorrect beliefs about them! We keep resurrecting them and, as a result, we believe lies about our pain. That, in turn, gives way to labeling and eventually to walking in a wrong identity. Meanwhile, we default to our unique ways of coping.

What needs to die in your life? Nothing will be resurrected until a death of sorts takes place first. Do not delay the process! You can change your story line by making the following exchanges:

- Exchange your negative view of God for an understanding of who He *really* is.
- Exchange the negative labels that veil your self-perception and self-image for accurate descriptors of who you are in Christ.
- Exchange your inaccurate and misguided beliefs for beliefs that are guided by God's truths.
- Exchange negative self-talk for positive truths and affirmations.

To begin the exchange process, first look to what Scripture says about who God is in the midst of your pain. He is close to the brokenhearted (Psalm 34:18) and binds their wounds (Psalm 147:3). He is reliable and trustworthy (I Corinthians 1:9). Then, replace who you *thought* Him to be with who He *is*.

Second, exchange what you say about yourself by looking at who God says you are. The field of psychology asserts that coming up with "alternative labels" promotes healthy thinking. God has already given them to us!

Believe **this** about yourself . . .	Instead of **this**:
1. Made in [God's] image	Damaged
2. Chosen	Rejected
3. Free	Held in bondage
4. Wanted	Unloved
5. Worthy	Devalued
6. Fully loved	Loved conditionally
7. Successful	A failure
8. Fearless	Anxious
9. Courageous	Cowardly
10. Blameless	Guilty
11. Purposeful	Useless
12. New	Old and unable to change
13. Empowered	Helpless
14. One of a kind	Living in comparison

15.	Strong	Weak
16.	Victorious	A victim
17.	Holy	Tainted

Third, exchange your beliefs about yourself and the events that have affected your heart. This is time well spent. Write down what you believe to be true. Fact-check your narrative. How can you reframe the way you think about your life? In no way do I want to minimize what you may have lived through, but you can reframe your thoughts in such a way as to see events and experiences from a different perspective. For instance, what could you learn from a given episode that you would not have learned otherwise? This cognitive tool allow you to think more existentially and broadly than you would have done otherwise, giving you a big-picture perspective.

The field of counseling recognizes the "automatic negative thoughts" (ANTs) that we never question. To counter those, pay attention to your thoughts and negative labels. They are a direct result of your beliefs, which, for many of us, remain unchallenged unless crisis demands they be challenged. Your thought life can either work *for* you or *against* you. I am a living testimony that changing your ways of perceiving and thinking can in fact change your life.

Separate your experience from your identity. This is crucial! Here are some practical examples:

- Grief is not your identity. It is your experience, but it does not need to define you.
- Your child—including his or her successes or failures—is not your identity.
- Performance is not your identity, it is simply what you do.
- Abuse of any kind is not your identity, nor is it what defines you.

- Your prodigal child is not your identity; your child is making her/his choices because she/he has also been hardwired with volition.
- Sins of the past are not your identity, nor do they define who you are. (Your identity is separate from any consequences that may result.)

When you realize in a cognitive sense that what you have done or what has been done to you is not your identity, you will be able to walk through life with value and self-worth. Your life experiences have no doubt affected you, but they are separate and apart from who you *are*.

Fourth, change the voices you listen to. Self-talk is the dialogue in your mind that only you hear. Pay attention to what you tell yourself about yourself! It will lead to either peace or panic. Believing truth will lead to peace. This truth-telling inner voice says, "No matter what comes your way, God says you are more than a conqueror" (Romans 8:37). Not just a conqueror, but *more* than a conqueror! You are the only one holding yourself back from moving forward. God already has a plan to use your painful experiences for His glory. We must recognize that Christ's victory over death gives us victory in life. And for us to have victory in life is to walk in a new identity.

Unveiling a Spiritual Takeaway

God has given you the gift of dominion (Genesis 2:15). You are not a victim of life's circumstances. The same power that raised Christ from the dead is available to you (Ephesians 1:19, 20).

Unveiling Questions for Discussion

Exchange

- How do you respond in light of your painful life experience(s)? Do you tend to default to . . .
  - Unhealthy behaviors? (e.g. emotional eating, spending, or other addictive behaviors)
  - Unhealthy thinking?
  - Both?
- Do you think God is close? Distant? Involved? Detached?
- Is your God image the same as the one you have of your earthly father?
- When you reflect on hard times, trials, life stressors, etc., what man-made, self-imposed labels automatically come to mind? Did other people impose their labels on you? What were they? Did you assume these labels to be true?
- When you truly absorb the meaning of Christ's death in the "glorious exchange," how can you exchange your negative labels for the ones that identify you as a daughter of the King of Kings?
- How can you reverse, redeem, or repair your perceptions? What needs to change in your thinking?
- How would your destiny look different if you made these exchanges?
- How would you like your story to end? What steps are necessary in order for your story to end this way?

Identity Unveiled Promises and Reflections

You are a *new creation* (2 Corinthians 5:17).

      What's the "old" that needs to go?

You have a *new way of looking at your circumstances* (1 Corinthians 2:16).

      What's a better, healthier way of looking at your life?

You have been *redeemed*, so what needs to be reversed (Ephesians 1:7)?

      What can you do to change a family pattern?

You are totally *accepted* (Romans 15:7).

      Since God accepts you 'as is,' what obstacles are preventing you from accepting yourself?

You are *free from accusation* (Colossians 1:22).

      What new self-affirmation from Scripture releases you from Satan, the accuser?

You are *free from condemnation* (Romans 8:1).

      For what do you need to stop condemning yourself?

Your experiences are not wasted; rather, they are used for a greater good to reflect God's glory in your life (Romans 8:28).

CHANGE YOUR STORY!

Part III

WHO I AM!

Chapter Seven

WHAT'S IN A NAME?

But by the grace of God I am what I am and
his grace to me was not without effect.

1 Corinthians 15:10

All the days ordained for me were written in your book
before one of them came to be.

Psalm 139:16b

Therefore, if anyone is in Christ, he is a new creation.

2 Corinthians 5:17a

Allow me to circle back in recapping my identity. I was born a nobody, unwanted by the king. I had no birth certificate to identify me. My certificate of identification (shown on the next page) wasn't even issued until the month I went to live with my parents, May 1963. And, then, I was simply known as a Persian "Jane Doe" with the name Firoozeh Kaviani Monfared. Translated, *firoozeh* means blue or turquoise. My mother told me the nurses in the hospital where I was born gave me this name because of my blue eyes. I believe it is not coincidental that the gold ring given to me by the Iranian national who arranged my adoption contains turquoise stones.

RAHIM HAKIM

8, PASSAGE IRAN
LALEZAR AVE.,
TEHRAN - IRAN
TEL. : 35069

OFFICIAL TRANSLATOR
TO THE MINISTRY OF JUSTICE

دارالترجمه ر . حکیم
مترجم رسمی وزارت دادگستری
خیابان لاله زار - پاساژ ایران
تلفن : ۳۵۰۶۹

Translation from Persian.

Iranian Emblem "Lion and Sun."

Ministry of Interior. The Administration of Identification.

Copy of Identity Certificate.   Serial No. Sad/573572

Date of issue of the copy of Identity Certificate: 5/8/1343.

Specifications of the holder of Identity Certificate:

Identity Certificate No. 80063 issued at the Fourth Ward of the Bureau

of Identification of Tehran.

Date issued: 4/3/1342.

Name: Firoozeh,   Surname: Kaviani Monfared.

Father's Name: Unknown.   Mother's Name: Unknown.

Birth Date: 19th. Mehrmah 1341 (11 October 1962)

Birth Place: Tehran.   Domicile: Tehran.

This certified copy of Identity Certificate was issued without any

error or omission and was delivered to the Chief of Fulbereit, residing

at Charrahe Amir, No.1530.

Signature and Seal of the Bureau of Identification of Tehran.

(Signed and Sealed)

True translation of the original. Official Translator to the Ministry

of Justice. Rahim Hakim.

~90~

My anonymity continued when, upon our departure from Iran, I was issued an "alien" registration card. I wasn't legally known as Shirene until my adoption in 1966. I was naturalized a year later:

Regardless of the ascribed labels I was born with and the labels that ensued later, the name that God gave me stood before the man-made ones. God has declared you His own and has given you an identity that transcends your life experiences and any negative labels resulting from those experiences. Here is what God says about your new name, which also gives you a new purpose and mission:

Yet to all who received him, to those who believed in his name, he gave the right to become children of God—children born not of natural descent, nor of human decision or a husband's will, but born of God.

John 1:12, 13

God seeks you out to reverse your destiny, just as He did for me! Allow your past to be incorporated into your new mission. John Ortberg writes in his book *When the Game Is Over It All Goes Back in the Box*: "You did not get to vote on your parents, your birthplace, your family order, or your DNA. All of these were chosen for you. You were made the bearer of a human soul, created in the image of God, destined for an eternal existence" (p. 186).

God wastes nothing in your life or in mine. He intends to use your strengths, weaknesses, sins, dissatisfactions, and all of the hardships in life to feed into the greater plan and destiny on this earth that only *you* can fulfill. God is responsible for the outcome of your mission, not you. You are simply the messenger with the message that He has given your heart.

Unveiling a Spiritual Takeaway

In Christ, you are no longer the person you used to be. You have the power and capacity to change your perception of your life's experiences. Your identity is not your experience. You have been made new on every level—spiritually, relationally, and emotionally.

Chapter Eight

A PREORDAINED PURPOSE

For we are God's workmanship, created in Christ Jesus to do good
works, which God prepared in advance for you to do.
Ephesians 2:10

Destiny appoints one but affects many.
Beth Moore, *Esther*

To miss out on the mission he gives is to spend our entire lives
trying to win the wrong game.
John Ortberg,
When the Game Is Over It All Goes Back in the Box, p. 180

While living in Tehran, my mother was a radio talk show host for AFRS, whose listeners were American military wives. Household tips, interviews with military personnel, recipes, and popular music were weekly features. After I went to live with my parents in May 1963, Mom dedicated the popular song *More* (Theme from Mondo Cane) to me on the air. Its opening line is fitting for the love God has for you and me: "More than the greatest love the world has known . . ." Because of this love displayed on the cross, He wants you to know the truths of who He is and who you are. His death, burial, and resurrection weren't just payment for *your* sin, they were also meant to overcome the pain, sin, and loss that would keep you from living victoriously. He wants that former pain to be dead and buried, never to be resurrected again!

God wants *more* for you! He wants you to embrace the backstory over which you had no decision or control. He wants you to change your personal narrative by knowing of His love for you and acknowledging your *real* identity—chosen, loved, redeemed, accepted, victorious, valued, fearless, and worthy. If you take these truths and plant them in the deepest places of your heart and mind, then healing, assurance, and confidence will guide you into your future.

If God has given you a new identity, which He has, then Scripture also indicates He has given you a mission on this earth while you are here. I will go so far as to say that the mission God has given you has picked you! You are the messenger based on *who* you are, *what* your backstory is, *what* you have been through, and whether you have had to *rewrite* any chapters in your narrative. God stands above time and knew the plan He had for you before you were born. Why? Your life mission is actually *not* about you, but about God and others. Do you need to remove the veil of pride in your life that prevents you from sharing your experiences and embracing the mission that God has for you?

I recently spent time with someone whom I had not seen in quite a while. She indicated she was done being inauthentic with others regarding the issues her heart struggles with. Shouldn't we all be done with that? Don't we all want to be our authentic selves by sharing our passions, deepest satisfactions, and painful experiences to encourage others? When you realize where your true identity lies, then sharing will come easily because you will not be worried about what others think. Insecurity focuses on self; security focuses on God. It's His story, remember? As long as you are obedient in sharing your story with others who need to hear it, then how they interpret the events of your life and how you have responded to them becomes their issue, not yours. You are called to obedience. God is responsible for the outcome, not you.

Unveiling a Spiritual Takeaway

Only you can fulfill the destiny that God has preordained for you since before your birth.

Chapter Nine

FOR HIS GLORY

We do not dare to classify or compare ourselves with some who commend themselves. When they measure themselves by themselves and compare themselves with themselves, they are not wise.

2 Corinthians 10:12

No man and no destiny can be compared with any other man or any other destiny.

Viktor Frankl

During the Iranian Revolution of 1979, statues of the shah toppled to the ground while the people of Iran revolted against his policies and ideals. He had erected images of himself so his subjects would be clear as to who had authority in the land. He wanted his image to be familiar to his subjects and to engender an aura of respect that often accompanies fame.

According to God's perfect design, each person is to reflect the image of the King of Kings, because He is the Creator of each unique life. Some people acknowledge the presence of God in their life, while others do not. Those of us who acknowledge God as their Father reflect God's image in our lives through our personal backstory and the ways we have changed our story to be based on truth rather than lies. Then, we are tasked with the task of sharing our journey with others to reveal and reflect His glory.

Problems often arise when we are too busy trying to live others' lives without living ours. Nothing will kill your self-worth and confidence more than comparison. In today's social media age, the pitfalls of comparison are all too clear. Comparing has become so automatic that you may not even be aware you are doing it. Children and teens who lack the wisdom of life experience struggle under the weight of comparison all the more. The American educational system tells them what they are to study and what a smart student is to study in college. iPhone apps, social media, and peer pressure influence how they think they should look and act, and we wonder why depression and anxiety are at an all-time high!

A low estimation of your worth can be overcome by renewing your mind, as discussed in prior chapters. Your value is not determined by "likes" or how you see yourself in relation to others. Women, if you are mothers and grandmothers, you must fight the battle of comparison in your home. You have been given your children as a gift to "train [them] in the way [they] should go" (Proverbs 22:6). It matters not what other parents do. Have a single focus on the unique child or children God has given you. This verse implies the responsibility to nurture, guide, discover, and celebrate who they are! It is not just a call to spiritual guidance and influence. Stop playing the comparison game. Your children are not to live or look like you, your other children, their friends, or what society claims to be worthy or valuable. Furthermore, do not try to live vicariously through them. They have their own strengths, passions, and abilities. They are not here to live out your unfulfilled dreams. They are created as you are—to reflect the image of their Creator.

Once you replace your negative, never-challenged labels, your image of yourself will be accurate. You will then be able to reflect the image of God in your life.

But whether or not you live out your life purpose and point others to God through your life story is up to you. Choose wisely. You have one chance. The past is not relevant. God is ready to begin a new work in your life today. The Holy Spirit's voice of truth will show you how every single detail in your life has been orchestrated to conform you to Jesus' image. Unfortunately, it is usually through the hardships that our image changes. The problem is that it is easy to hold on to pain rather than surrender it. And when we cling to our pain, we cannot see how any good can come from it. This makes perfect sense. As long as we hold on tightly—as did the members of my family—we will never walk in the identity that we were created for. The experiences of life will define us. What we lack in self-worth and confidence, we make up for by staying stuck in the past, tied to the very thing or person that we are trying to run from. When you recognize that your negative experiences can be used for good, you will then see how God can use you to impact others' lives for the kingdom.

That, my friend, is why you are here.

Unveiling a Spiritual Takeaway

God assumes responsibility for your story's ending. Change your chapters if they need to be changed. In God's timing and under His watchful eye, He initiates change by using whatever means He can to lovingly prompt you toward change. He desires your obedience and cooperation to conform you to His son's image. Grab hold of your past, grapple with the present, and gain mastery of the future!

You are a Daughter of THE King of Kings!

Unveiling Questions for Discussion

Exalt

- How can God use the totality of your life your experiences, your talents, your passions, your personality—to accomplish His plan in your life?
- How can your *entrance* and *exchange* be used to *exalt?*
- Can you think of specific ways or venues to share your story?
- Who needs to hear it?
- Who would be encouraged by it?
- Would your story be shared best through mentoring? Teaching? In a group setting?
- How can you point others to God as you share your story with them?
- Point to specific examples in your life of how God has redeemed, restored, and renewed.
- How can your new identity become your destiny? Can you see how your old identity is also incorporated into your destiny?

FOR HIS GLORY!

Identity Unveiled Promises

I = God made me for a specific purpose that is *individualistic* and *incomparable.*

D = It's not what I do, but what Christ has already *done.*

E = God will not waste my life *experiences.*

N = I can change my *negative* perceptions with God's help.

T = God is completely safe, loving, and *trustworthy.*

I = My old self-image and my image of God can be exchanged for correct *images.*

T = I can use my God-given and acquired *talents* as I share my life experiences with others.

Y = I can say *"yes"* to being available for His purposes.

THE LAST WORD

WHO AM I?

I am . . .

. . . the story I tell myself when pain and disappointment have interrupted the story line I had hoped for.

. . . the story that writes itself without getting fact-checked.

. . . the unexpected chapter that shatters my confidence and worth.

. . . the "happily ever after" page that has been drowned in tears and is no longer legible.

. . . my wounds!

And here is where the story line changes . . .

His words and my words, His wounds and my wounds are superimposed on the cross.

Consistent with God's loving nature, as revealed in the Bible, I imagine Him speaking to me and to you:

"I was convicted so you wouldn't condemn yourself."

"I was shunned so you wouldn't be separated from my love."

"I was declared guilty so sin would never define you."

"I was denounced so you would walk in worth."

"I grieved so you could be renewed."

"I became death so you could live again."

"I breathed my last so my Spirit could breathe new life in you."

"I wore a crown of thorns so you could hold your head high."

"I slumped to my death so you could stand tall."

Sister in Christ, because of your identity as a child of God, neither the past nor the present are the ending. *GOD is responsible for how your story ends.* YOU are responsible for the chapters that are still being written and for the way you handle those written in your past. Do not be afraid to embrace your pain and disappointment, as doing so equips and empowers you to write a new and better life story. Hold your head high and share your personal words that others need to hear.

When you unveil your true identity, you can live in the fullness and joy that come with being a daughter of the King of Kings!

CHANGE YOUR STORY LINE!

EPILOGUE

My journey of discovery has led me to a surprising conclusion about my origins. There is no need to further prove my earthly parentage. The lens through which I viewed myself and my family history has been replaced by a different understanding of where I came from. Just as the gold ring I possess displays the seal of the Pahlavi family, my faith in Christ is the seal that assures my membership in the family of God. Without a doubt, every experience I have had in my lifetime has made me the person I am today. I thank God for using everything I have been through to bring me to an understanding of my spiritual parentage and to reveal an exhilarating truth: I am His!

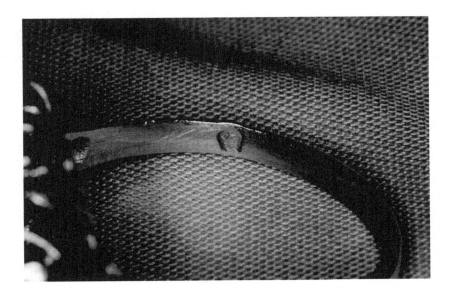

SEALED BY THE KING

Unknown for years your seal I carried,
A jewel of authenticity for who I am?
Your ephemeral reign veiled with insecurity
A history you claim.
The identity that now defines you.
Am I yours? Am I yours? Am I yours?

Known forever, Your seal I carry on my heart,
An inheritance of ownership for whose I am.
Your imperishable reign veils me with assurance
A narrative I claim.
The identity that now defines me.
I am Yours. I am Yours. I am Yours.

Made in the USA
Monee, IL
09 December 2019

18223930R00066